CONSIDERING THE WOMEN

Choman Hardi was born in Sulaimani and lived in Iraq and Iran before seeking asylum in the UK in 1993. She was educated in the universities of Oxford (BA, Philosophy and psychology), London (MA, Philosophy) and Kent (PhD, Mental health). She was awarded a scholarship from the Leverhulme Trust to carry out her post-doctoral research about women survivors of genocide in Kurdistan-Iraq. The resulting book, *Gendered Experiences of Genocide: Anfal Survivors in Kurdistan-Iraq* (Ashgate, 2011), was chosen by the Yankee Book Peddler as a UK Core Title.

Hardi has published collections of poetry in Kurdish and English. Her first English collection, *Life for Us*, was published by Bloodaxe Books in 2004. In 2007 one of her poems from this collection, 'My children', was featured on Poems on the Underground in London. In 2010 four poems from the same collection were included in the English GCSE curriculum in the UK (AQA and Edexel). In August 2014, another poem, 'Summer Roof', was chosen by London's Southbank Centre as one of the '50 greatest love poems of the past 50 years'. In November 2014 she was awarded The Woman's Prize by Andesha Cultural Centre in Sulaimani for her academic and creative achievements. Her latest English collection, *Considering the Women* (Bloodaxe Books, 2015), a Poetry Book Society Recommendation, was shortlisted for the Forward Prize for Best Collection in 2016

She has been poet in residence at Moniack Mhor Writers Centre (Scotland), Villa Hellebosch (Belgium), Hedgebrook Women Writers' Retreat (USA) and The Booth (Shetland). As an academic researcher she has been a visiting scholar in The Centre for Multiethnic Research (Uppsala University), Zentrum Moderner Orient (Berlin) and The Department of Humanities (University of Amsterdam). Between 2009 and 2011 she was a Senior Associate Member of St Anthony's College, Oxford. In 2014 she moved back to her home-city of Sulaimani to take up a post at the American University of Iraq (AUIS), becoming chair of the department of English in 2015.

CHOMAN HARDI

CONSIDERING THE WOMEN

BLOODAXE BOOKS

ISBN: 978 1 78037 278 5

First published 2015 by
Bloodaxe Books Ltd,
Eastburn,
South Park,
Hexham,
Northumberland NE46 1BS.

Second impression 2017.

www.bloodaxebooks.com
For further information about Bloodaxe titles
please visit our website or write to
the above address for a catalogue.

Supported using public funding by
**ARTS COUNCIL
ENGLAND**

Cover design: Neil Astley & Pamela Robertson-Pearce.

Printed in Great Britain by Bell & Bain Limited, Glasgow, Scotland, on
acid-free paper sourced from mills with FSC chain of custody certification.

ACKNOWLEDGEMENTS

Acknowledgements are due to the editors of the following publications where earlier versions of some of these poems first appeared: *Poetry Review, Ploughshares, Washington Square, Modern Poetry in Translation* and *Exiled Ink!* 'As Clouds Slide Across The Sky' was published on *Connaissances* website under the title of 'Sometimes'. 'Adila's Apple' and 'Before You Leave' were included on the Poetry Archive CD: *Choman Hardi reading from her poems*. The poems and title of 'My English Years' are indebted to Rob Cole.

I am forever grateful to Jane Duran, whose poetry workshops were an education and a continual source of inspiration for me and for reading this collection and giving me feedback and support.

I am also grateful to John Glenday who read and commented on earlier versions of some of the poems in the *Anfal* sequence. Thanks to Vicki Feaver, Clare Pollard and Susan Pearce who generously gave feedback on the translations in this book. Clare Shaw was brilliant with the *Anfal* sequence and responded to it with passion and sensitivity. Special thanks to my dear friend Lucy Williams who read the whole of this collection and responded to it.

I am grateful to the Leverhulme Trust for a two-year scholarship which made it possible to research the experiences of women survivors of genocide in Kurdistan. I have drawn on this research for the *Anfal* sequence in this book as well as on the Middle East Watch Report, *Genocide in Iraq: The Anfal Campaign Against the Kurds* and Kanaan Makiya's chapter on Anfal in *Cruelty and Silence: War, Tyranny, Uprising, and the Arab World*. The details of the survivors' stories have been changed.

CONTENTS

11   Before You Leave
12   Memory Bias
13   Crossing Back
14   The Maths Lesson
16   A Woman Before Her Time
18   Homeland, What Shall Do with You?
20   One Moment for Halabja
21   The Silent Visit
22   A Man's Honour
23   The Heroes

ANFAL
27   Preface: Researcher's Speech
28   The 1984 Negotiation
29   Gas Attack
30   Escaping Kanitu, March 1988
32   Arrest at Milla Sura
33   Dibs Camp, the Women's Prison
34   The Child at the Pits
36   The Elderly from Nugra Salman Camp
38   The Gas Survivor
39   Dispute Over a Mass Grave
40   The No-Survivor Village
41   The Angry Survivor
42   Researcher's Blues

45   Her Autumn
46   Istikhara
47   Your dress
48   Bawka
50   Unanswered
51   The New Bedroom
52   Adila's Apple

53   The Housewarming Gift
54   The Seventh Wedding Invitation
55   My English Years
55   *Divisions*
56   *The Picture*
57   *Conversations*
58   *Our Different Worlds*
59   *My English Years*
60   Time Out
61   Shetland, 1469
62   Leaves
63   As Clouds Slide across the Sky
64   His Blue Sky
65   The Three Dancers, 1925
66   The Couple
66   *The Husband*
67   *The Wife*
68   Blackout
69   Flights
70   A Day for Love

Before You Leave

(thanks to Jacob Polley's 'Moving House')

Wrap your language in plenty of silk,
each word separated from the other
so that they don't rub, get scratched.

Don't forget the words you never use,
as years go by and details fade
you may need them.

Take a suitcase
full of your thirsty mountains,
they will thrive in that rain.

Pack the voices of your neighbourhood
in a musical box, firmly locked
for the long journey.

Take the debates of the male intellectuals,
their passionate fights, books full
of their arguments.

Carry your mother's warmth in your skin,
her smell in your clothes.

Your father will always be with you
each time you take a step,
make a decision, or refrain.

The widows' cries, miscarried
children, and the creeping cancer will remain
in your dreams, you won't miss them.

Drag your schools behind you as you go,
the begging benches,
the crying lessons.

Memory Bias

(for Bzhar Alladin)

He will forget the summer dust, landing
on his school books, making his hair
stand stiff. He will forget the winter wind,
his aching toes, his tender bones.

He will forget the ragged roads, the endless
promises to fix them. He will forget the black-
outs, wordless nights without music
when he is unable to do his homework.

He will forget how petty everything is,
how he tastes disappointment every day.
What he will remember is the fine spring days
when green is a gift, the gleaming rain

on the dusty roads, and his mother
when she is in a good mood.

Crossing Back

The fact that you left is certain
but when exactly did you cross back?
Was it when you were tickled by your language
once again? When a childhood song intruded,
stayed in your head all through your dreams?

You thought you had left the arid mountains,
were free from the violence of the roads.
You thought you did not care any more.
When did you let it slip back into you,
making you bleed from restlessness?

Now you stand before the wind, considering
the women. The women who suffered yesterday's
politics, rebuilt the mountains stone by stone,
who made, gave birth, nurtured, aged.
The women who are silenced, beaten, slain.

The Maths Lesson

TRANSLATED FROM KURDISH

It was an innocent morning, Miss Shanaz!
In the year four class of a heartbroken school
the door's back was broken, the window
cracked from sorrow. Outside, a high wind
howled and we sat on our hard benches –
two to three students to a bench – trembling.

But on that morning, using a question
as excuse to bring Jhala to the blackboard,
you suddenly asked her about her sister,
murdered by her father a few weeks before.
You committed a crime, Miss Shanaz, when
in front of thirty students, you made Jhala cry

with your endless questions. Her hands
started to shake but you didn't let it go.
You were looking for details to tell your friends
in the teachers' common room as you had tea
and cake. She cried and we were stunned,
listening. She wiped away fat tears,

turning towards the blackboard in shame,
so we couldn't see. 'Who are you crying for?'
you asked her. What a senseless question!
Even we children knew that she cried for her sister,
not her father. After that lesson, after that day,
every time I saw Jhala I was speechless, because

after your questions a girl in the class told me –
that night when her father was strangling her,
Jhala's sister put her finger between her teeth
in order to breathe. The girl also told me when
she had eventually died, her index finger was left
behind in her mouth. All that year the bitten-off

finger of Jhala's sister and the bruised fingerprints
of her father on her neck stayed in my mind.
Until the end of that year, every time I saw Jhala,
her shaking hands and big tears came into my mind.
What a crime you committed, Miss Shanaz!
You turned the Maths lesson into an interrogation

session full of fear and panic: fear that if we don't
listen to our fathers, we too may be strangled,
our thin fingers left behind in our throats, and after our
deaths, one innocent morning our little sisters may be
grilled with questions – in class, in front of their friends,
made to cry to the point of breaking.

A Woman Before Her Time

(for Ahlam Mansur)

A VERSION OF A KURDISH POEM

You were a beautiful beginning,
full of words' radiance, ideas' ignition.
The only female voice amongst the men,
they were all ears when you spoke,
all eyes when you showed up.

You loved bravely, wrote honestly,
lived up to your ideals, swam against
the tide. You were a rebellion,
a promise of freedom, unequalled
if only the nation could see.

Your people did not kill you for 'honour'.
They did not want to make a martyr of you.
Bit by bit, stage by stage they killed you.
They first silenced you,
then they threatened you.

They turned you into a joke, laughed at you.
They considered you sick, a mad woman.
Then they gave you up to loneliness, left you
alone. Their disrespect killed you,
fear and isolation killed you.

The men of this country –
some in the name of love, feigning
openness yet full of honour's stones,
some in the name of religion, their hands
washed for prayer, their mouth full of *fatwa*,

some in the name of friendship, their ears
eager, their mouths full of gossip,
some in the name of literature
with smiley faces and critical lips,
some in the name of politics, apparently liberal –

all had a hand in your slow murder.
Anyone who once inhaled your sorrow's
smoke, witnessed your frightening loneliness,
had remotely known of your heartbreaks,
should have known that the day would come

it will quickly come, you would
suddenly leave us without a word.
The day came dada Ahlam, you left us.
It is too late to drink a bitter tea with you,
tell you how, as young women, we delighted

in your existence. We have no time left
dada Ahlam, we woke up too late.
After you left us we all started writing
poems, articles, confessions; took your wake
to a mosque, a place whose men were against you.

This nation which until your last days
was full of hard words and war
is now asking for your forgiveness.
This nation is doomed to regret
because it never learns a lesson.

Its longest commemoration is a couple of days
then it picnics, forgetting what has just
happened, where it is heading, what it should be
doing. We were late dada Ahlam
as usual we are very late. You left early.

Homeland, What Shall I Do with You?

TRANSLATED FROM KURDISH

*In February 2014 the decaying bodies of two sisters were found
in a pond 12 days after their death. Photographs of the police
pulling the sisters out with rope shocked everyone. The bodies
were dragged on the floor, destroying evidence. Later the invest-
igation found no trace of abuse. Apparently the two sisters had
committed suicide. They were 18 and 16 years old.*

By the murky pond
in which the two sisters drift
look at your policemen.
Look at the ropes in their hands
and tell me if these men hunt fish or mermaids.
Are they saviours or offenders?

Look at the crowd, coming to watch.
Look at their keen eyes and cameras.
Look how much they yearn for blood,
blood and images of blood,
abuse and images of abuse,
self-immolation and its images,
rape and its images.

Might this be the dictator's fault –
caused by his blood-filled cells,
his gassing our souls, his slaughter of freedom?
Might this be the heritage of violence,
which has turned us into a people
who know no mercy, feel no guilt,
and are never shocked?

Might it be the revolution's fault?
Caused by glorifying murder,
the rituals of aggression?

Might it be caused by brilliant lies
and endless promises?
By liberation's rape and the fall
from grace of its revolutionaries?

I don't know, homeland!
The excuses are numerous
and women are numerous.
Force and violence are brothers
and women are alone.

Homeland! You are still
drenched in blood in my dreams.
Tell me how can I fix you?
Which crime shall I tackle?
Which wound shall I bandage?
You tell me, where shall I start?
What shall I do to make you change?

I can't turn my back on you
to carry on as you are.
With what will you change?
The pleading mothers,
angry streets, and endless analysis
did not change you.
What shall I do with you, homeland?

What shall I do with all this blood?
Where shall I put you
to prevent you from filling my days
with damage and grief?
Where I shall I put you, brutalised homeland?
You tell me, where shall I put you?

One Moment for Halabja

(to honour the victims)

TRANSLATED FROM KURDISH

One moment of no silence, no sorrow.
One moment of thinking not of your entangled,
twisted bodies, your blistered eyes,
your poisoned blue lips.

This time, one moment of applause for your
remembrance, dear ones. One moment
of smiling. One moment of thinking
of your dreams, colourful as finches.

One moment of standing, not in front of
the pictures which turned to stone
your shattering. This time one moment
of standing to pay respect

to the people who wanted to live longer,
to those who were scared and those who weren't,
those whose hearts were full of kindness
and those who were cold-hearted,

to you, all of you, from the old to the young,
to you who used to walk the streets,
remembering yesterday,
and thinking of tomorrow.

The Silent Visit

(thanks to Welat Zeydanlioglu)

In the buzzing room in Diarbakir prison
words are thrown back and forth
rushing out to beat time, short enough
for more longing. The old woman
sits amongst the crowd in silence, watching
her son who stares back at her with no words.
She wishes she could hold his beaten hand
hoping that touch could convey
her love to him. Above their heads
a large sign reads: *Türkçe konuş, çok konuş* –
Speak Turkish, speak a lot.

A Man's Honour

(thanks to kak Ahmad Eskandari)

She is plump, smiley, blushing as if
in embarrassment. In extra large traditional
dress, she is apologetic for being larger
than life, larger than him and his tribe.
He walks erect, his head held high,
his chest sticking out, while she trails
behind, anxious not to disgrace him.
That part of her body where it all happens
is faithfully hidden beneath layers of clothing –
an old pair of pants, thick baggy trousers,
her undergarment and then her flowery dress.

The Heroes

They come on TV yesterday's heroes
boasting scars, bullet-marked limbs, pigmented
skin. Every spring the martyrs resurface,
scruffy and bright eyed on the large posters.
The old hymns are replayed and the broken bodies
of the children displayed. Rows of fighters
climb a mountain and the voice over says:
'These are the people who brought us today.'
Today when there is no more myth,
no more faith in black and white.

ANFAL

Between 23 February and 6 September 1988 the Iraqi state launched a genocide campaign against rural Kurdistan. The campaign targeted six geographical regions, destroying over 2000 villages, killing 100,000 civilians and displacing many more. Besides conventional bombing, 281 locations were gassed during the campaign. The majority of the victims ended up in mass graves. Some civilians died of starvation and illness in the prison camps while others died during the bombardments and gassing or during their flight to Iran and Turkey.

Preface: Researcher's Speech

I have come to learn about your pain,
fill me up with your words. I have not been
gassed, nor imprisoned, not mothered children
to watch them starve or wither away, don't
know what widowhood feels like. I have not
lived in a shack, nor worked hard in
fields and factories to bring food back.

I want to document your suffering, make sure
your voice is heard. I cannot promise redress
or direct help. But I promise to listen
with all that I have, stay true to your story,
not distort or edit your grief. I will write
a book, try to bring you acknowledgement.
So let's begin, tell me about your life.

The 1984 Negotiation

In the one-year peace an endless picnic
unfolded, smoke wrapped around the mountain-
side, spreading the smell of dolma, grilled meat.

Colourful sequins gleamed in the bright
light as men and women held hands and danced.
In one of these picnics, enwrapped in this hope

I fell in love with a dangerous man
who carried a gun, loved a good fight.
An itinerant, he wore khaki clothes

kept a long beard, but had a boy's bright
smile and brazen eyes. I left the comforts of
my village, followed him deep into the mountains.

I served the revolution by washing the men's
clothes, cooking for them, bandaging their wounds,
giving birth twice. I didn't realise

that three years on we would all get caught up
in it. No one fled. No one imagined
such an end. The cruelty caught us by surprise.

Gas Attack

Badria Saeed Khidir and Ayshe Maghdid Mahmud

Bombs could fall anywhere, any time of the day.
They were a nuisance we got used to. In our
dug out shelters we felt safe, until that haunting

winter twilight when the muffled explosions
deceived us. We came out thinking we'd survived
the bombs but a chalky-yellow powder settled

on our skin, smelling of sweet apples at first,
seemed safe to breathe in. People were going crazy –
laughing, buckling at the knees, twisting, running

to the water source, blinded, bumping into trees.
Villagers from the region came to our aid. They said
my son looked strange, as if his eye-colour had spilt

out, his face was blistered, blackened. He groaned
like a calf faced with the knife. I was still blind when he
died, could not see him, did not say goodbye.

Escaping Kanitu, March 1988

Najiba Ahmad and Fatima Muhammad Amin

Everything began to end that winter. Inch by inch
we withdrew, stopped at Kanitu, prepared for the caves –
baking bread, boiling meat, sorting through clothes.

Then someone screamed: 'They're coming.' We left
the bread on the saj tray, the meat on the kerosene
heater, the clothes in their bundles and fled.

What thick rain! You could not see one metre ahead.
And you know how it is in the cold country, when it
rains in the valley it is snowing in the mountain.

Climbing up we were bashed by wind, bombarded by snow.
People began to throw away stiffened blankets, useless
weapons, bags of bread, books, photos in their pockets.

A couple who carried three children on their backs,
abandoned one. It was a boy, was he four years old?
He didn't sway, too numb. Maybe dead.

A wounded peshmarga zipped himself up in a sleeping bag
and said: 'Goodbye', the flakes rapidly covering him up.
Four hours on we gave up the climb, started pulling away.

Then I saw the dead bodies standing. One was my cousin's friend,
eyes open, stuck in snow up to his chest.
I called his name twice, hoping he would come with us.

At the bottom people lit a fire with abandoned things.
A child they had given up on, started weeping after
her jaw thawed. Only then I began to pray. The next day

we headed to the border on the back of mules till Iranian cars
picked us up. We arrived in the first village, got out of
the car, fell to the floor, could not stand on our feet anymore.

Even now the frost doesn't leave me alone, cripples me
on cold winter days. The doctors say it is psycho-
logical. Do they mean that when I strain to stand, to hold
a spoon or open a door, I am just remembering my old pain?

Arrest at Milla Sura

14 April 1988

The crimes that would be, were lurking
at the beginning of that day. The rising sun
was dipped in blood. We had a sense
of our own ruin but could not turn back.

The planes were circling overhead but not
shooting, the army was led by jubilant Kurdish
mercenaries. Thousands of us were walking
the banned road in broad daylight, no one came

back. We were transported to Topzawa camp
by IFA trucks. The whole of Kurdistan was
stranded there, caught up in its filth and fear,
its selections: women and children to one side,

old people to the other. Men and teenage boys were
stripped-down, their pockets emptied, eyes covered,
hands tied behind their backs. If you had seen
how they were kicked into the windowless trucks

you would have known where they were taking
them, you wouldn't have wondered whether they
were coming back. What was left of them? Combs,
beads, mirrors, IDs, piled, soaking in the rain.

Dibs Camp, the Women's Prison

Nabat Fayaq Rahman

You do not die! Not when you want to.
Not when you see your strong husband, the big
brother in his own family, kicked bloody by a group
of men equipped with loaded guns and hatred.

Not when your beautiful teenage daughter
is handpicked by soldiers, never comes back.
And for the rest of your life you are left to wonder:
was she sold to prostitution? Does she still live?

Not when your son withers in your lap
and he cries until he can no more, when the last thing
he asks of you is 'cucumber', and you give him
a green slipper to suckle on, because he is beyond

knowing the difference. No. Not even when
the rest of your children grow fed up with
your black garments, secret tears, headaches
when you smell cucumber. You do not die.

The Child at the Pits

Taymour Abdullah, the twelve-year-old boy who survived.

This is how it happened: in Topzawa they stripped
the women of their earrings, rings, took the babies' milk
bottles, told us there was no need for things where
we were going, crammed us into ambulance-shaped
trucks, with small windows at the back – women and
children, no men, no old people. Then began the journey
on the long desert road, passing Arab villages on the way.
People had come to the side of the street, ululating
in celebration. I saw a boy, probably my age, who slid
the tip of his fingers across his throat. A pregnant woman
fainted inside the truck from heat, thirst, lack of oxygen.
For the most part we were on a main road then we hit
the dirt. It must have taken twelve hours or more.
Then the trucks stopped, the doors flung open, they
grabbed us by the limbs and dragged us out. I saw the pits,
too many of them, they smelt fresh. The bulldozers
were on standby. They lined us up, the pit behind us
and the soldiers in front. I can't remember what everyone
said, there were whispers, some were stunned, some too
exhausted to make a fuss. I was with my mother and three
sisters, my aunt and cousins, few hundred villagers.
The officer ordered: fire! And the soldiers shot.
I was wounded but not badly. I got up again, grabbed
the soldier's arm, begged him not to shoot. Then I saw
that he was crying. The officer ordered to shoot again,
and then he did. This time I laid low. The soldiers went
away and I saw that my mother and sisters were dead,
blood spurted from my aunt's wrist. A young girl was still
alive, not wounded. I told her to run away with me
but she did not dare. I crawled out of the pit, hid behind
the dirt mound and kept going until I reached the last grave
which was still empty. I must have passed out. When I
woke up it was all quiet. The soldiers had gone, the pits

were covered up with dirt. Then I ran as fast as I could,
promised God that should I survive, I would give
five dinars to the poor. At dawn I reached the Bedouin
village, where the dogs surrounded me with their barks.
Till someone came with a torch, took me into a tent.
They treated my wounds, protected me, taught me
Arabic, accepted me like one of their own, but that is
another story, I will tell it to you another time.

The Elderly from Nugra Salman Camp

'This is Hell, they told us, you have been brought here to die.'
— Haji Ali, February 2006

What shall I tell you about Anfal? Shall I start
by saying that my four sons, five daughters
and their twenty-four children disappeared?
Shall I tell you how much I have thought
about how they were killed? Did they sell
the pretty girls? That is what we heard.

My old wife and I were separated from them
in Topzawa. The soldiers shouted orders
we did not understand. They dragged the men
out, pulled us to the side, left the women and children
screaming in the middle. My young grandson
walked towards us, two soldiers slapped him

all the way back to his mother. Had they let him
stay, he may have survived. I started crying
in Topzawa. I knew it was the end of everything
we had built. Do you have children? Then
you don't understand how much work
is put into raising one child, let alone

nine. It was as if all that we had woven in
forty years was being undone. Our life
was undone, our hopes, our futures. We
had hoped to die in our own homes, surrounded
by children and grandchildren. We trusted
that we would not outlive them,

that things would continue as they were,
as they should have. We ended up in Nugra
Salman. Have you seen pictures? It was hell.
We lost the battle to lice, filth and sickness,
gave up promptly burying the dead, saying
a prayer, observing the rituals of a wake.

When men and women stronger than us
kept falling all around, it was a miracle
that we survived. Was there a point in our
survival? We wish there was. Shall I tell you
about our food and water? The sweet water tank
that came once a day, giving each of us a small flask

which should have lasted the day? The alternative
was salty water from the well, which some of us
drank in desperation and got sick and died.
Our daily food was three dry buns, you broke your
tooth on them. If you had money you could buy
things at inflated prices from the guards.

If you were poor like us, you just ate what you got.
Shall I tell you about Hajjaj? The lieutenant who
beat us every day? How he forced us into the heat
of the summer courtyard? We who had lived our lives
in the cold mountains? Once he tied up three men
to electric poles in the blazing heat. When they were

taken off, the skin of their backs remained on the poles.
Or maybe I should tell you about the black dog
who dug out the dead bodies from their shallow
graves and ate them. I saw my cousin's clothes
in his mouth, the ones we had buried him in.

The Gas Survivor

Badria Saeed Khidir, Nakhsheen Saeed Osman and Rabia Muhamad Ibrahim

My body is blooming. Every night leaking flowers,
I turn my mattress into a bed of roses – black,
cherry-red, pink and gold. By day I hand-wash
the towels, recall the stillborn after the gassing.

Who would have thought there are weapons
that turn every part of your body against you?
Every bruise, cough, or nosebleed seeming like
the final betrayal? Weapons that turn you into

a despised being in your own village, no one
daring to visit you, thinking you are contagious.
Weapons that kill you years after being exposed,
leaving you unable to blame anyone for your death?

Dispute Over a Mass Grave

The one you have finished examining
is my son. That is the milky coloured Kurdish
suit his father tailored for him, the blue shirt
his uncle gave to him. Your findings prove
that it is him – he was a tall fifteen year old,
was left handed, had broken a rib.

I know she too has been looking for her son
but you have to tell her that this is not him.
Yes the two of them were playmates and fought
the year before. But it was my son who broke
a rib, hers only feigned to escape trouble.

That one is mine! Please give him back to me.
I will bury him on the verge of my garden –
the mulberry tree will offer him its shadow,
the flowers will earnestly guard his grave,
the hens will peck on his gravestone,
the beehive will hum above his head.

The No-Survivor Village

Who remembers Omer Qala
at the tip of Zarda mountain?
Who remembers the lives that unfolded
there, the lives that are no more?
Who can believe that they all died –
men and women, old and young?
Who can recount their apprehension,
their doomed efforts to escape?
Who knows how they were killed –
the surrender, the trucks, the desert
road, the mass graves? Who knows
about their thirst, their last bloody
wish? The wide eyed children
in the back of trucks, waving
at civilians, unaware of their fate?

The Angry Survivor

I am fed up with documentations of my grief –
journalists asking me to sing a lullaby for my
dead children, to broadcast during commemorations,
government officials using my story as propaganda
during elections, women activists forcing me to talk
about rape only to prove that women are oppressed,
researchers claiming to record history when
all they do is pick my wounds.

This is my story, not yours. Long after you
turn off your recorder I stay indoors and weep.
Why don't people understand? I am neither hero,
nor God, cannot stand the talk of forgiveness.
For years I went to every wake. Wept at every man's
funeral. Kept asking: Why? Realised I will never
understand. Now I just endure the days, by planting
cucumbers which you interrupted, by believing

in another world where there is justice, by watching my
remaining children as they sleep. Spare me your despair
and understanding. You can't resurrect the dead, feed
my hungry children, bring me recognition and respect.
Take history with you and go. Don't come here
again, I just don't want to know.

Researcher's Blues

Every day I try to lose them in the streets,
leave them behind in a bend in the road and keep on
walking. But they follow me everywhere, their voices
combining into a hum from which sentences rise and fall.
The woman I never interviewed cut the string of my sleep
at dawn, whispering: 'I am not well'. Why didn't I listen
to her story? Why didn't I realise that she was dying?
The one widowed at 26 told me, 'Imagine twenty
years of loneliness.' I remember her in the middle of
an embrace and start weeping. The pleading voice
of the woman who was raped echoes in my head:
'I only wanted bread for my son.' I wish I had told her
that she is good, she is pure, not spoiled as she thinks she is.
Then I remember the old couple in their mud-brick house,
surrounded by goats and chickens. I remember their tears
when they talk about their children, when they remember
a woman who had been rich and powerful in her own village
but in Nugra Salman 'she was stinking, abandoned,
worm-stricken'. What was the dead woman's name?
Why didn't I try to find her family? I keep walking away.
All I want is to walk without crying, without being
pitied by people who think that I have problems
with love, without the homeless man telling me that he is
sorry. I want to disappear, be unnoticed, unpitied.
Sometime ago when I started, it was all clear. I knew
what had to be done. All I can do now is keep walking,
carrying this sorrow in my soul, all I can do is
pour with grief which has no beginning and no end.

Her Autumn

In her mother's back garden the large fig tree
stood alone, with dark leaves that prickled her fingers.
The morning shadow at its feet was pure and spotless
like her faith, her belief in fairytale endings.

Unlike the tree her perspective lived through
thirty years of spring, her optimism bore fruit –
she touched the wounded creatures of her homeland,
she loved them better and they loved her back.

Autumn came in her mid-thirties when the fig tree
had already died. She realised late that evil wins
much of the time, that bad things do happen to good
people. Then she was ready for the blows
for all the good people in the world to disappoint her.

Istikhara

The old woman silently watches her daughter
whose dimmed eyes speak of surrender.
Every day she gives her up to the streets,
to the heartening sunshine which should help.

This is her seventh child, the one she
spoiled with experienced mothering,
protected from cold, hunger, harm
but she could not protect her from this.

She takes her ablution before bedtime
and makes another deal with God.
She prays for a dream
one that would answer her question.

She dreams of fruit – a sweet watermelon
in her garden, a tall thick tree, its branches
heavy with bursting figs.

Your dress

You wore that dress forever, it seems –
I see you baking bread in it,
weeding the garden, hand-washing clothes.
It was brown and shiny with beige flowers,

each attached to a large green leaf.
You wore it until it curled round the edges.
It became shorter but still shone on you.
I sometimes smell your dress

when I cook and clean, rushing to make
things seem effortless. I smell it on my
bare skin – all your youth and strength.

Bawka

Bawka! I watched you swing your feet
at parties, your jaw locked, your bright eyes
staring forward. I heard you curse, talk to yourself,
outraged by the smallest things. I saw you laugh
from your heart, making wry jokes, surprising
everyone. I saw you cry.

They deemed you irrational for demanding
the four corners of your torn homeland.
But even those who despised you,
those who saw you as a threat, respected
you. Your hands remained clean,
your name spotless.

All my life I was embarrassed by your honesty,
your lack of tolerance for nonsense, how harsh
you were with people yet how much they loved you!
I memorised your poems before I could read,
before I knew how good they were, before I
realised that everyone recited, sang them.

All my life, doors opened to me because I was
yours and how you laughed when I told you:
I will make you famous one day.
How depressed you were, how angry!
You! Little man with small hands and feet
and huge eyes.

I watched you in shame when you dwelled
on being stateless. How your dark vision and fits
of rage angered me! Bawka! You were a mountain,
its size becoming apparent at a distance
and I was too close. How sad I am that you
did not see me in this language,

could not understand the music of my words!
And after all these years how similar I have become
to you, how I cry and curse and shout about
homeland. How harsh I am sometimes!
Just like you, Bawka!

Unanswered

The question was born, danced off the page
of a history book. It waved its arms,
started shouting, demanded an answer.
After keeping her awake for a few nights
it gradually gave up, froze on a sheet,
slowly sank to the bottom of her mind.
Then one day another question was born
out of a poem by Nali. She didn't call
to ask for help, just made a note.
She thought she had prepared for this,
it was not premature, nor unexpected.
But as her questions multiplied,
fighting for space on the white page,
she realised how final his loss was –
Her father, that small body, forever silent.

The New Bedroom

It was a dark, large room, two small windows
by the ceiling where the rim of the garden could be seen.
No golden sunsets or moonlit skies.

'The girls should have the basement,' he said,
'where no one could peek as they dressed and danced.'
But soon he was glad of this discrimination –

it was the coolest room in summer, warmest in winter.
It was a place where, away from father's eyes and mother's
complaints, he smoked the white walls yellow

and played his music loud, a place where the first
love letters were written to the girl he later married
and brought in as the woman of the house.

I visit the room now, smelling of damp and grease,
remember its days of glory. He doesn't notice, too busy
reading, writing books, talking about saving the world.

Adila's Apple

(thanks to Ersano Pargasori)

They had gone to look at Adila's apple –
the wholeness of it, how she held it in her hand
like a precious little moon. Usually
they each got one fourth, maybe a third
if they were lucky. Even then they argued
about whose slice was larger than whose.

But there she was, smelling of medicine
in her small bed, smiling as she raised it
in the air to show her cousins how lucky
she was – it was worth being sick for.
'The smell,' she said, 'the smell it gives
to my clothes.' It stayed in the chest
until it was rotten.

The Housewarming Gift

(thanks to Vénus Khoury-Ghata's 'Without the wisteria')

The garden arrived in a package one morning
after a vigorous knock on the door.
The young woman unwrapped it with sleepy eyes –

The trees marched out reciting the anthem,
they stomped their roots into the ground,
raised their branches as if in salute,
imposed their shadows all around.

A cheerful flock of sparrows flew out
concurrently singing the latest gossip,
a white butterfly trailed behind,
silent, sensitive, bashed by the wind.

The grass unrolled itself on the ground
covering the earthworms that sprained as if
in pain. At once the daisies jumped on the grass
which groaned and sighed as they giggled.

The roses walked out swaying their hips,
the reds and pinks bullying the yellows,
their scent imbuing the air she breathed

The erect marshmallows took their time,
they planted themselves on the sandy verge
each flower looking in a different direction
each of them hosting a buzzing bee.

The Seventh Wedding Invitation

Dear friends and family,
I promise this will be my last wedding
if it doesn't work out, I will just live with
another man, no more pledges. So please
come along to this final ceremony with a man
who, at the moment, fills my eyes. Do not
bring any more presents – pura Shahla's
non-stick pan is still in the box. Mama Hama's
gold ring has not been put on. And the naughty
lingerie will be worn for this man since my ex
was orthodox. He did not last. Do come along.
I promise to wear something more sophisticated
than a wedding dress. It is another chance to meet
and talk about Ama's failure in brining up
her children, to shed light, one more time,
on Layla's divorce, and Nina's remarriage
to her brother in law. We will have a fun night.
I have told my new man so much about you
and it may be your only chance to meet him.
With all my love, your little Lala.

My English Years

Divisions

All night as you slumbered
I thought of the rain at our windowpane –
the constant drumming, the water's rhythm.
Did you let the drops into your dreams?
Were they making daffodils in your head?
These were the things that divided us –
The rain, the music, what keeps us awake.

I listened all night and remembered
a place where the rain makes a difference –
helping the green to grow, filling gaps
in the ground. I took in your flow
and smelt your skin, all dewy then.
I wanted to share your peace and not let
the cold night come between us.

The Picture

We'd stopped for a picture on the cliff.
The green sea at our back, we'd stared forward
smiling at the stranger who photographed us.

You'd arched sideways to reach me
and I'd raised myself to my toes
to rest my head on your shoulder.

Later I would blame the photographer
for not warning me about my wild hair,
concealing your bright eye.

Stretching ourselves to reach other
seemed effortless then, the pull towards the middle,
difference and distance sliced with a hug, a word.

Conversations

At some moment a long time ago
our conversation was like a good game
of pingpong. We were face to face,
alert to each other's every word, responding fast.

Then, somehow, the space between us swelled,
conversation slowed, words became sleepy,
cold, bland. I carried on telling you about
my dreams, hopes, nightmares,

you responded in short sentences, sometimes
a smile, a nod, a shaking of the head. It took
me a while to realise that you'd stopped
talking, that you kept a lot to yourself.

Our Different Worlds

I went back in search of a nation
and found fragments instead –
tribes, regions, dialects, religions.
I went back to make a nation and came
back dispossessed, full of partitions.

You didn't understand why I left
you, our home, the beautiful streets,
flew through the night in a crowded plane
to a place where everything is sanctioned –
water, power, wealth, love.

And I took the bumpy unpaved roads
to villages full of ghosts of the lost
to listen to women I didn't know
talk about how it all happened,
why it continues. You didn't understand

why I kept going back to the dust and ruin,
to all the broken hearts that broke my heart.
You were fed up with victimhood,
you said, fed up with me because
I could not be happy.

And I was unable to explain why
I kept going there to listen and listen
till all my dreams turned into nightmares,
and my lovemaking just absent sharings
of an exhausted body.

My English Years

I discovered the beauties of Devon with you –
the single-track roads that marched forward
windy and winding, sheltered from the sun
by hedgerows, trees,

the open-hearted hills of Dartmoor
their granite tops forever grey,
the peaty fields that bounced back,
the Dart estuary at Dartmouth.

I observed the rituals of Christmas with you:
champagne at 12, lunch at 1, Queen's speech at 3,
tea at 5, opening presents in between,
sipping our wine as the tree twinkled.

I didn't know at the time that those were
my English years, when I spoke your language,
listened to your music, read, wrote and made love
in English. I didn't know that the past

was sleeping inside me, gathering strength,
waiting to strike. I didn't think a day would come
when homeland would wake up in my heart
and like a beast in a childhood dream

it would summon me to its ruins
and enchant me. I couldn't imagine
that I would leave you and not turn back.

Time Out

Sit back from the world and watch the sea
as it shivers in the rain, flees from the wind,
rewinds itself. Notice how it reflects the mood
of the sky, looks up to the moon, taking cues from it –
to invade the coast or retreat in defeat. Remember
how it esteems the dead, holds them high above
its head, how flirtatiously it lures travellers in,
dangerous even when it stands still. The pains
you have caused will always be here, the losses
you feel will never be redressed. And this is only
the beginning – you may live to see the end of those
you love. You may be left alone in a wheelchair,
watching the sea by the window as the rain strikes.

Shetland, 1469

Land locked in the North Sea,
silver sea at the end of the day,
a blend-in horizon between sea and sky,
the endless sky in every direction,
the peat – thousands of years in the making,
hills standing in defiance to the wind,
the unchained wind spinning the mills,
the people with their open hearts.
This is what they gave away
as the dowry of a princess.

Leaves

Can you see the leaves, each fresh and lively
shivering on their stems? Do you notice
how they turn left, right, left again?
Like a synchronised army of soldiers
they sway, sending waves up the height of the tree.

Have you noticed how the branch tips
are lost in greenness, up there, where the broody rook
has laid her eggs? In autumn the trees go blonde,
so delicate that a mild wind can undress them.
How graciously they fall, following each other,
piling up, crunchy under our feet.

As Clouds Slide across the Sky

She says, Sometimes we glorify
a dead person, a short love affair.
Sometimes, she says, we glorify a person
because they are dead. We long
for an affair because it was short.

Today is the day, she says,
There is no point in missing this sunshine
by remembering another.
No point in thinking yesterday was fine
when this moment is.

But as the clouds slide across the sky
she thinks of him, of that cold Christmas night
when she stayed awake to watch him sleep.
There is no point, she says,
no point but she thinks of him.

His Blue Sky

His eyes were full of blue sky
his lips were sweet from wine.
The day our closeness made us cry
his eyes were full of blue sky.
I can't change things however I try
he would never be mine.
His eyes were full of blue sky
his lips were sweet from wine.

The Three Dancers, 1925

(Picasso)

The flawless woman stands on one foot
holding the men's hands up
in a dance that she leads.

The man on her right, half brown half white,
seems to be blind. His shadow
larger than he would ever be.

On her left the other man is abstracted,
broken into fragments. He bends
backwards with music in his heart.

Behind her back they still
hold hands, a timid hanging on
to a friendship long gone.

The Couple

The Husband

They are everywhere. I cannot escape
the girls I fathered, their adorned mother,
her grumpy cur and the women who help.
In the dark, damp corridor the paintings
and prints mockingly stare back at me.
For a split second I think I can see my
father in the brightened doorway. He is
about to leave me with all that I have made.

They think it is easy to lead this life –
to spend my days changing cold colours
into meaningful shapes. And every night
as moonlight streams into the chamber
all I think about is how to avoid my wife's embrace,
avoid making another girl, another copy
of her mother, greedy for food and love,
staring at me with needy eyes.

The Wife

He used to love making babies, but only
boys – invaders, inventors, rulers, thinkers.
Five daughters later, his hopes faltered.
Now it is nonstop work. He thinks the maids
do it all. As if this large household needs no
supervision from me. As though maintaining
relations with his buyers, their tedious wives,
is easy work. Without me he would hardly

sell, being arrogant and proud, past his prime
with colours. He comes to bed late to avoid me.
I pretend to be asleep, face the wall and think
of the times when I desired him. When he was
the young artist who created, ventured, lived
for the two of us. Every night as he dreams
of freedom I am sleepless, wondering how
we managed to create all this unhappiness.

Blackout

You are lying down on the flat roof
on a hot summer night and suddenly a blackout.
It is as if the house holds you up to the sky
which shines its stars for you.

The man you love is still downstairs
trying to bring up a jug of iced water.
You know that he will stretch his arm out,
slide his feet, tread cautiously,

uncertain of the room he knows so well,
as though it is possible for furniture
to move about and trick him.
He will trace the edge of the counter

and notice that it is chipped
he will feel the coolness of the fridge door,
pull it open. He will be surprised
because its light does not come on.

It is all a small betrayal, like life going wrong –
a house disappearing after a bomb,
a loved one not waking up from sleep,
villages being erased from a map,
all the ruptures that cannot be explained.

Flights

I have flown many times, over the harsh landscape
of my homeland, parched for the lack of rain, peace,
beheaded forests, scorched mountains struggling to hold on
to their trees, fields holding their breath for spring.

I have flown over many lands, some heartbreakingly
beautiful like Bosnia where the dead were killed twice –
they were killed, buried, uncovered, killed again
each part of the body buried in a different grave.

Over places where beside the lavish buildings
poverty walks all over the streets, in ragged clothes,
places where despite the struggles of the past,
hope and happiness are woven every day.

But none resemble the flights I take with you
when we break away from wars, famine, suffering
and nothing exists but us, weightless in each other's
arms, looking down at ourselves in surprise.

A Day for Love

TRANSLATED FROM KURDISH

This is the day for love, the day not to think
of wars, to tell violence: 'we have had enough,
stand in the corner on one foot', give poverty
a loaf of bread so that it can snooze, warn oppression
to be careful: 'An oppressor is on the way.'

This is the day to remember
our first kiss, the first whisper,
the smell of your hands in the lavender garden,
the youthful rain, lush behind you and your oblivion
as you drenched yourself in the colour of my eyes.

We have this day for gratitude
so that I can thank you, thank God that you
are mine. Thanks for all the mornings when we
enclose our daughter like closed brackets
and I want to cry.

Please don't steal the day from us. Don't
tell us about the girl who was murdered in her sleep.
Don't show images of the foetus, shot dead inside
her mother. Don't tell us about the stupidity of leaders,
the folly of politicians, the brutality of humans.

We want to hold on to this moment today,
to think about love's voice, colour and taste.
Please leave this day to us. And don't worry,
tomorrow we will roll up our sleeves once again,
we will listen out. We will be here

to write another letter against oppression,
to sign another petition against injustice.
But today, let us be, to consider our love.